FOOTBALL

A PUZZLE BOOK FOR THE 2022/23 PREMIER LEAGUE SEASON

Test your knowledge of football.

This crossword puzzle book has been designed for football fans young and old.

Can you complete all 20 puzzles?

Each team in the Premier League this season has a crossword puzzle to solve, with questions about the players, the teams, and the clubs in general.

As always, the answers are at the back of the book (but no peeking until you're finished).

We've made every attempt to ensure the information is accurate and up to date for the 2022-23 season at the time of printing.

Unless otherwise stated, answers are a single word and player names usually refer to surnames. If a player's name is two words it will either be first name and last name, or there may be two parts to the last name.

CROSSWORD PUZZLES

ANSWERS

ARSENAL

ACROSS:

3. When Arsenal went unbeaten on their way to winning the title in 2003/04, what special version of the Premier League Trophy was presented to them (4)
5. Swiss central midfielder who has been sent off five times for Arsenal in the league (5)
8. Arsenal's home ground, The _____ (8)
10. English winger, who scored 11 goals in the league in the 2021/22 season (4)
11. New Portuguese signing from FC Porto, Fabio _____ (6)
13. Manager in charge when Arsenal last won the Premier League (6)
15. This young defender help to keep thirteen clean sheets in the league last year (3,5)
16. Arsenal are based in this area of London (5)

DOWN:

1. Norweigen maestro (8)
2. Arsenal's first opponent in the league in 2022/23 (6)
4. Arsenal's new Brazilian striker signed from Man City (5)
6. Where Arsenal finished in the league last year (5)
7. Goalkeeper signed from Bournemouth (8)
9. Dominant Brazilian central defender (7)
12. The item on Arsenal's crest relating to their nickname 'The Gunners' (6)
14. Arsenal beat this team 5-1 on the final day of the 2021/22 season (7)

THE GUNNERS

Founded: 1886
Based: Islington, London
Stadium capacity: 60,704

1
2
3
4
5
6
7
8
9
10
11
12
13
14
15
16

ASTON VILLA

ACROSS:

2. New defensive signing from Sevilla, Diego ______ (6)
4. Villa's captain last year (5)
5. Scottish midfielder at Villa since 2018 (6)
9. Shot stopper who kept 11 clean sheets last year (8)
12. Who scored in last season's 1-0 win over Manchester United (5)
15. Villa's top scorer across the Premier League with 73 goals (10)
16. The last English trophy Villa won was the _______ cup (6)

DOWN:

1. Top goalscorer last year (7)
3. Creative left back, previously at Everton (5)
6. Brazilian playmaker (8)
7. Another nickname based on the clubs colours... The _______ and blues (6)
8. City where Aston Villa are based (10)
10. The only club to have spent longer in the top flight than Villa (7)
11. Villa's most expensive signing from Norwich (7)
13. Name of the home ground _____ Park (5)
14. Despite his name, the oldest player at the club (5)

THE VILLANS

Founded: 1874
Based: Aston
Stadium capacity: 42,749

1
2
3
4
5
6
7
8
9
10
11
12
13
14
15
16

BOURNEMOUTH

ACROSS:

4. Shot stopper who kept 20 clean sheets last season (7)
6. Last year's top scorer with 29 goals (7)
9. Head coach, Scott _____ (6)
11. Scored the final goal of last season against Milwall (5)
12. The county Bournemouth are based in (6)
13. Before 1971, Bournemouth were known by this name (8)
15. Bournemouth's final position in the 2021/22 Championship table (6)

DOWN:

1. Bournemouth’s home ground The ______ Stadium (8)
2. New right back signed from West Ham on a free (10)
3. Striker who scored 67 goals for the club, now playing for a rival Premier League team (6)
5. Who are The Cherries’ biggest rivals? (11)
7. Record transfer signing in 2018 from Levante (5)
8. This centre back was sold to a Premier League clue for a record £41,000,000 in 2020 (3)
10. What the A stands for in AFC Bournemouth (8)
13. Danish playmaker previously at Huddersfield (7)
14. The main colour of Bournemouth’s kit (3)

THE CHERRIES

Founded: 1899
Based: Kings Park, Boscombe
Stadium capacity: 11,364

1
2
3
4
5
6
7
8
9
10
11
12
13
14
15

BRENTFORD

ACROSS:

2. Home ground up until 2020 ______ Park (7)
3. Scored a hat trick against Port Vale in the FA Cup (6)
8. Danish head coach, formerly at Brondby IF, Thomas _____ (5)
9. Top scorer for the club in 2021/22, scoring 12 goals in the league (4,5)
12. New signing from Hull. Double-barrelled surname (5,6)
14. German midfielder scored twice against Chelsea (6)

DOWN:

1. New goalkeeper signed on a free from Lazio, Thomas ______ (9)
4. Algerian winger who scored 30 times for Brentford before leaving in January 2021 (8)
5. English striker who moved to Villa in 2020 for over £30,000,000 (5,6)
6. Scored the first goal of the 2021/22 season in the win against Arsenal (5)
7. Clean sheets Raya kept in the league in 2021/22 (5)
10. Defender with 5 goals in all competitions in 2021/22 (5)
11. Norwegian defensive midfielder (8)
13. Creative midfielder who registered 4 assists in just 11 games in the league in 2021/22 (7)
14. Ethan Pinnock plays for which national team (7)

THE BEES

Founded: 1889
Based: Brentford, London
Stadium capacity: 17,250

1
2
3
4
5
6
7
8
9
10
11
12
13
14

BRIGHTON & HOVE ALBION

ACROSS:

1. Which tall defender left for a Premier League rival in January 2022? (4)
4. Which national team does young striker Aaron Connolly play for (7)
5. Brighton's head coach, previously at Swansea (6)
7. The main man between the sticks (7)
9. Striker who scored the final goal of the 2021/22 season in the win against West Ham (7)
11. Man on the match in the 4-0 victory over Manchester United in the 2021/22 season (7)
12. The two colours Brighton are known for (4,5)
14. Falmer Stadium is also known as The ____ (4)
15. New German striker, Denis ____ (5)

DOWN:

2. Where Brighton finished in the league last year (5)
3. Brighton's biggest rivals... nicknamed the A23 derby (7,6)
6. From which Belgian club did Brighton sign Trossard for £14.4 million (4)
8. How many goals Lewis Dunk scored in the league in the 2020/21 season (4)
10. Brighton's top goalscorer with 123 goals in 209 appearances from 1922-1929, Tommy ____ (4)
11. Spanish left back, who had a breakthrough season in 2021/22 (9)
13. New attacking signing from Libertad, Julio ____ (6)

THE SEAGULLS

Founded: 1901

Based: Falmer, Brighton and Hove

Stadium capacity: 31,800

CHELSEA

ACROSS:

2. Most expensive transfer in the clubs history, costing almost £100 million (6)
3. Played the most minutes for Chelsea in 2021/22 (5)
4. Penalty master (8)
7. Number of Premier League titles won by Chelsea (4)
8. Registered 9 assists in the league in 2021/22 from wingback (5,5)
10. This shot stopper cost a world record £71 million _____ Arrizabalaga (4)
12. Home ground (8,6)
14. Another nickname for Chelsea, The _____ (10)

DOWN:

1. Which midfielder missed Chelsea's final penalty in the FA Cup final in 2021/22 against Liverpool (5,5)
3. Which English player scored a hat trick against Norwich in Chelsea's 7-1 victory (5)
5. Midfielder who impressed at Crystal Palace on loan (9)
6. Who scored the winning goal in the FIFA Club World Cup Final in 2021/22 (7)
7. The manager of Chelsea's first opponent this year. Also a club legend (5,7)
9. The oldest member of the first team squad (5)
11. Who Chelsea beat 2-1 in the FIFA Club World Cup Final in 2021/22 (9)
13. Scored the last goal of the 2021/22 season against Watford (7)

THE BLUES

Founded: 1905
Based: Fulham, London
Stadium capacity: 40,834

1
2
3
4
5
6
7
8
9
10
11
12
13
14

CRYSTAL PALACE

ACROSS:

3. Teenage French attacking midfielder (5)
5. Top goalscorer in the 2021/22 season, with 14 goals in the league (8,4)
7. The most expensive player in Palace's history. Joined in 2016 (7)
10. First name of young English defender _____ Mitchell (6)
11. Veteran Scottish central midfielder (8)
12. New midfielder who signed for £19 million from Lens (8)
13. Started the most games in the league for Palace in 2021/22, Marc _____ (5)
14. The number of goals Mateta scored in the league in 2021/22 (4)
15. Scored in the win against Man United in the final game of the 2021/22 season (4)

DOWN:

1. Goalkeeper recently signed on a free (9)
2. Impressed in 2021/22 on loan from Chelsea (9)
4. Home ground, _____ Park
6. Manager and a legendary French midfielder (7,6)
8. French striker who joined Palace on deadline day in 2021 from Celtic (7)
9. The main colour of Palace's away shirt (5)

THE EAGLES

Founded: 1905
Based: Selhurst, London
Stadium capacity: 25,486

1
2
3
4
5
6
7
8
9
10
11
12
13
14
15

EVERTON

ACROSS:

4. English centre back, joined on a free from Burnley (9)
5. Which young midfielder scored in the 1-0 victory against Man United (6)
7. Top scorer in the 2021/22 season with 10 goals in the league (11)
8. The derby against Liverpool (10)
10. Everton's record purchase at just under £45million in 2017 (10)
12. Commanding central defender who scored 3 goals in the league in 2021/22 (5)
13. England international Jordan Pickford joined from which club in 2017 (10)

DOWN:

1. Everton > Chelsea > Man United (6)
2. Manager, previously played for Chelsea (7)
3. Which club legend took interim charge of Everton in 2019 and 2022 (6,8)
5. Home ground of The Toffees, ____ Park (8)
6. Which loan signing scored in the final game in the 5-1 defeat to Arsenal (3,2,4)
9. The 1995 FA Cup winning side were known by the nick name 'The ____ of War' (4)
11. Appointed as manager in June 2021 before being sacked in January 2022 (4,7)

THE TOFFEES

Founded: 1878
Based: Liverpool
Stadium capacity: 39,572

1
2
3
4
5
6
7
8
9
10
11
12
13

FULHAM

ACROSS:

4. Record signing from Nice in 2018/19, Jean Michael ____ (4)
6. The three letters on Fulham's badge (3)
7. First name of prolific Serbian striker (10)
9. French striker who scored 63 goals for the club before joining Man United in 2004 (4)
10. Defender who played every match for Fulham in the 2021/22 season (4)
12. Scored in the FA Cup third round 1-0 win over Bristol City (6)
13. Both played for (2013-2017) and managed the club (2019-2021) (5,6)
14. How many goals did Fulham score away against Reading in their 2021/22 Championship fixture? (5)

DOWN:

1. New midfield signing from Sporting, Joao ____ (8)
2. Fulham's captain. Scottish midfielder (7)
3. Who did Fulham sign Serbian striker Mitrovic from in 2018 (9)
5. New signing, known as the pre-season Pirlo (7,7)
8. Portugese head coach (5,5)
11. Scored a hat trick against Bristol City in the 2021/22 season (8)

THE COTTAGERS

Founded: 1879
Based: Fulham, London
Stadium capacity: 19,359

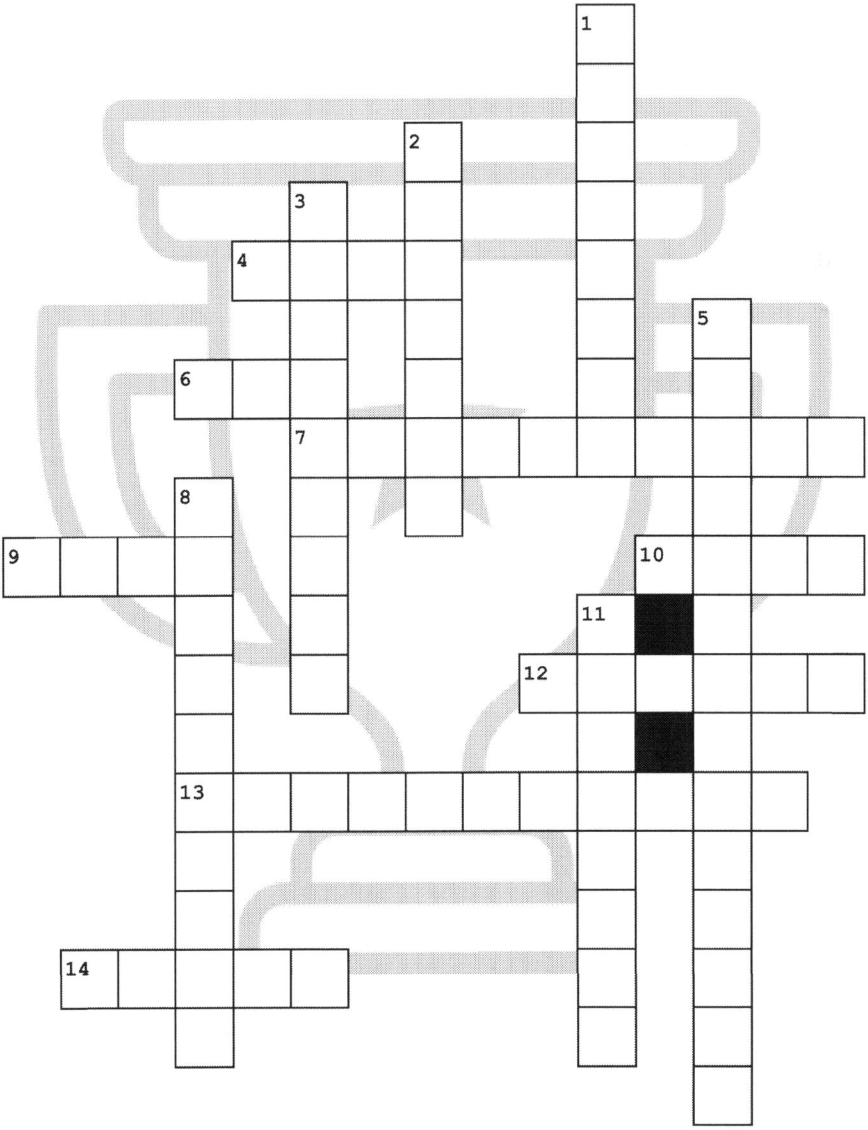
1
2
3
4
5
6
7
8
9
10
11
12
13
14

LEEDS UNITED

ACROSS:

2. Midfielder Kalvin Phillips recently joined from... (10,4)
3. Top scorer for Leeds in the 2021/22 Premier league with 11 goals. Now at Barcelona (7)
6. Fiesty Argentine manager sacked by Leeds in February 2022 (6)
8. How many times have Leeds won the FA Cup (3)
9. Ever present between the sticks in 2021/22 Premier League (7)
10. Scored the injury time in the final game of the 2021/22 season against Brentford (8)
12. Home ground since 1919 (6,4)
13. Liverpool player who started his career at Leeds in 2002 at 16 years old (5,6)

DOWN:

1. Which team knocked Leeds out of the Carabao Cup Fourth Round in 2021/22 (7)
4. Title of Leeds documentary on Prime, Take Us ____ (4)
5. Welsh winger who topped the assist chart in 2021/22 (6,5)
7. New signing from Red Bull Salzburg. American winger / midfielder, Brenden _____ (8)
11. Which defender scored the first goal for Leeds in the 2021/22 season against Man United? (6)
14. The American head coach (6)

THE WHITES

Founded: 1919
Based: Beeston, Leeds
Stadium capacity: 37,972

1
2
3
4
5
6
7
8
9
10
11
12
13
14

LEICESTER CITY

ACROSS:

2. Spanish forward signed from Newcastle in 2019 for £30million (5,5)
3. Leicester beat this 2nd place team to the league title in 2015/16 by 10 points (7)
5. Zambian striker who in 2021/22 scored 5 goals in the league and 5 goals in the Europa League (4)
7. Young midfielder who broke into the team in 2021/22 Kiernan _____ (8,4)
9. Foxes top scorer in the league in 2021/22 with 15 (5,5)
10. Leicester's home ground, The ____ ____ Stadium (4,5)
11. Explosive Algerian ex-Leicester winger now at another Premier League club (6)
14. Leicester legend who also loves a bag of crisps (4,7)
15. First name of Leicester's record signing who joined from Monaco in 2019 (5)
16. The club that Brendan Rodgers joined from in 2019 (6)

DOWN:

1. Young English defender who recently made his way back from injury (6)
4. Registered 10 assists in the league in 2021/22 (6)
6. His sale set a new world record for the transfer fee of a defender in 2019 (7)
8. Danish goalkeeper following in his father's footsteps (10)
12. In 2021 Leicester won this trophy for the first time (2,3)
13. Scored the winner against PSV Eindhoven in the Europa Conference Quarter Finals (7)

THE FOXES

Founded: 1884
Based: Leicester
Stadium capacity: 32,261

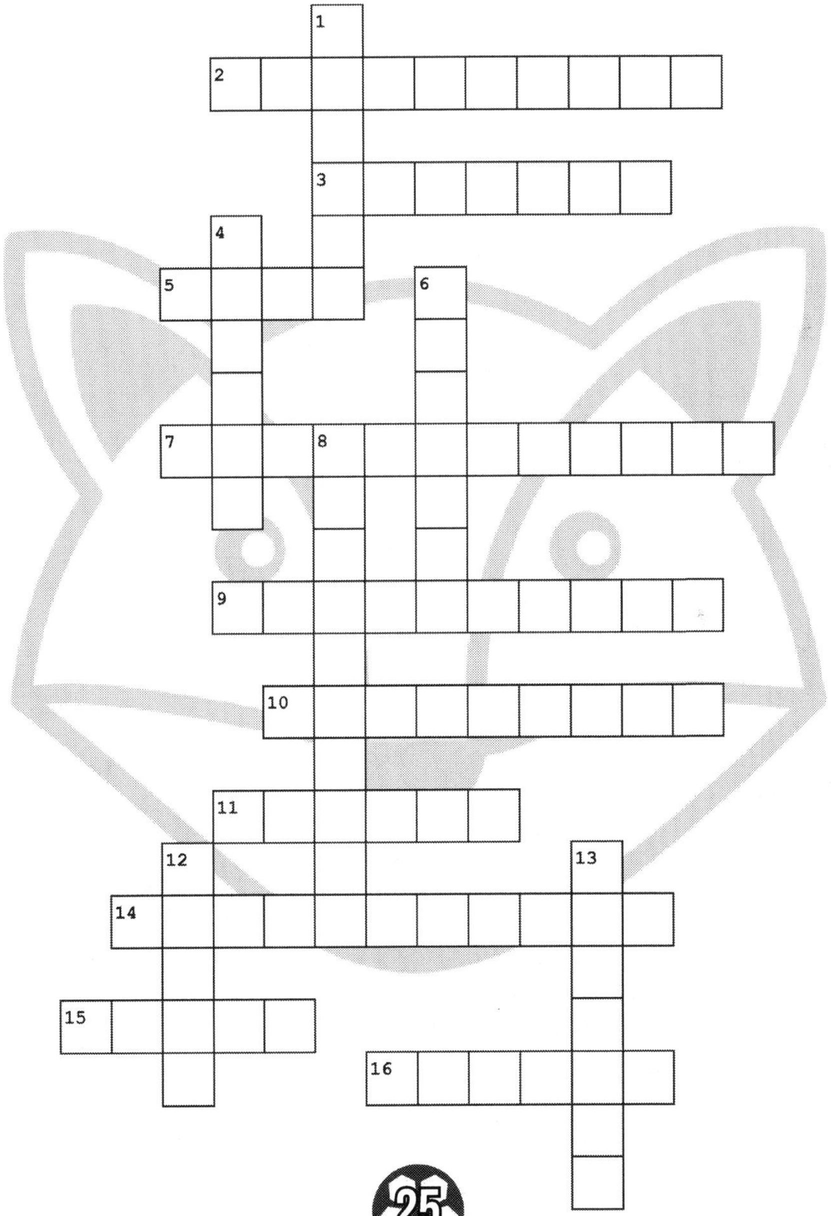
1
2
3
4
5
6
7
8
9
10
11
12
13
14
15
16

LIVERPOOL

ACROSS:

2. Young midfielder, recently signed from Fulham (8)
4. Keeper who scored Liverpool's final penalty in The Carabao Cup Final in 2021/22 (8)
5. One of the most successful January signings, joined in January 2022 (4,4)
6. Most expensive Liverpool signing to date (6,3,4)
7. Mane recently joined this club (6,6)
9. Scored Liverpool's penalty to win the 2021-22 FA Cup (8)
11. Oldest member of the squad who still offers a lot in various positions (5,6)
14. Scored the only goal in the 1-0 loss for Real Madrid in the 2021/22 Champions League final (6)
15. Managed Liverpool before Klopp joined in 2015 (7,7)
16. Team that Liverpool beat on 11-10 penalties in The Carabao Cup Final in 2021/22
17. Scored a hat trick against rivals in the recent 5-0 win (2,5)

DOWN:

1. Scored a brace in Liverpool's 2021/22
3. New attacker signed from Benfica (6,5)
8. Sold to Barcelona for over £120 million in 2017/18 (8)
10. When Salah wasn't on the pitch this midfielder scored 2 penalties in the league in 2021/22 (7)
12. Liverpool's top scorer of all time with 346 goals (3,4)
13. English defender. Assist king (9,6)

THE REDS

Founded: 1892
Based: Anfield, Liverpool
Stadium capacity: 53,394

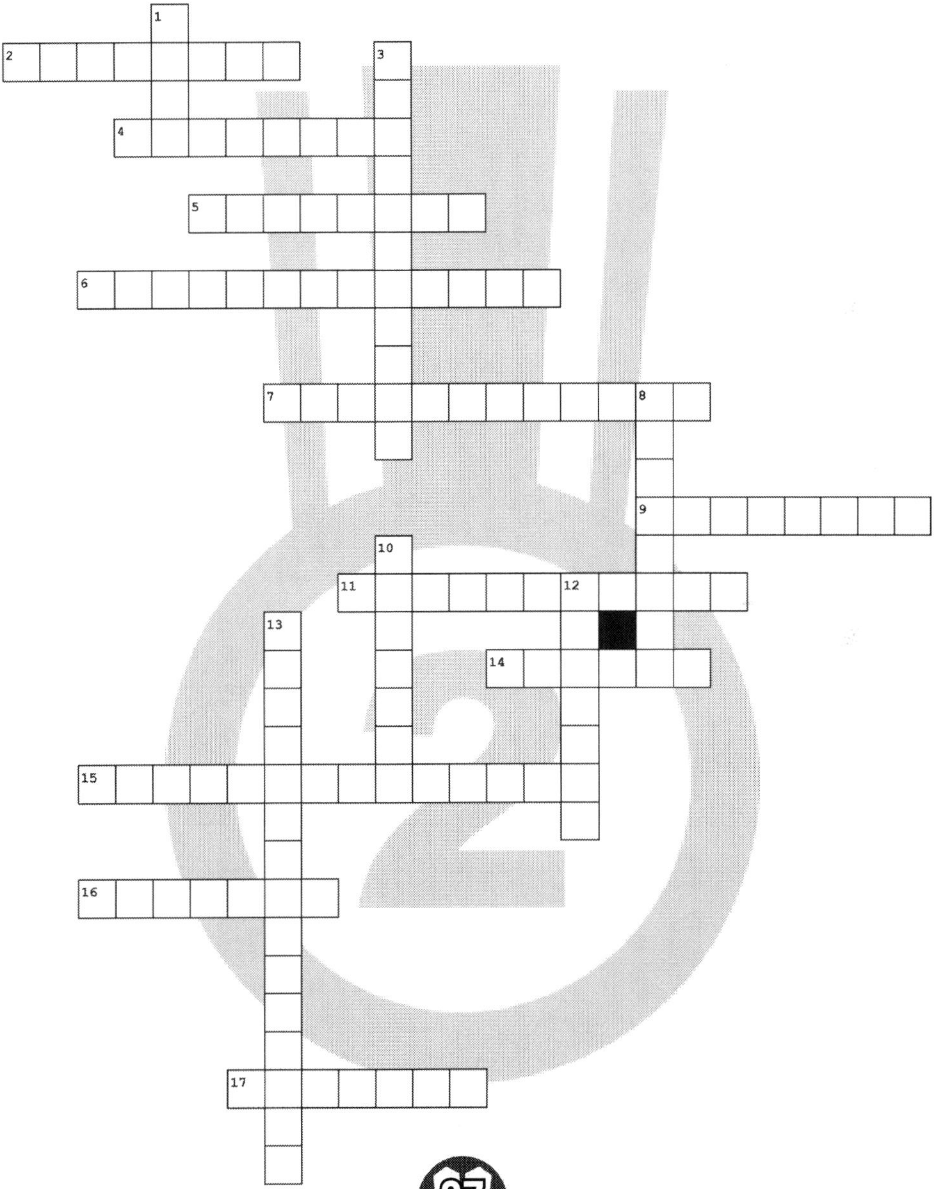
1
2
3
4
5
6
7
8
9
10
11
12
13
14
15
16
17

MANCHESTER CITY

ACROSS:

3. Song synonymous with City (4,4)
5. Brazilian who registered 8 goals and 8 assists in the league in 2021/22 (7,5)
7. The City of Manchester Stadium is also known as The ____ (6)
9. Top scorer in the 2021/22 league for City with 15 (2,6)
12. Liverpool > Man City > Chelsea (8)
15. Pep Guardiola joined City from which team in 2016 (6,6)
16. Portuguese defender. Offers a huge attacking threat (7)

DOWN:

1. Record signing for Man City at over £100million (4,8)
2. City first teamer born in Stockport (5)
4. Previously managed Man City. First name is Leslie (4,6)
6. How many goals City scored at home against Leeds in the 2021/22 Premier League (5)
8. New forward signed from Dortmund (6,7)
10. Record goalscorer for the club with 184 goals in the Premier League (6)
11. How many goals Kevin De Bruyne scored against Wolves in the 5-1 win in May 2022 (4)
13. Scored the winning goal in the 3-2 comeback against Villa in the final game of the 2021/22 season (8)
14. New signing. Impressed for England in Euro 2020 (8)

THE CITIZENS

Founded: 1894
Based: Bradford, Manchester
Stadium capacity: 53,400

1
2
3
4
5
6
7
8
9
10
11
12
13
14
15
16

MANCHESTER UNITED

ACROSS:

4. Top scorer for United in the 2021/22 season (7)
6. Started every game in the league in 2021/22 (2,3)
7. Made curtains a fashionable haircut in the 90s (7)
10. Inter Milan > Brentford > Man Utd (9,7)
11. Nickame of Old Trafford, The ____ ____ ____ (7,2,6)
14. The midfield duo of Fred and McTominay is refered to this by the fans (2,4)
15. Club owners, The ____ (7)
16. Ten Hag managed this Dutch club before joining Ajax in 2017 (7)
17. Won the 2022 Jimmy Murphy Young Player of the Year Award 2022 (8)

DOWN:

1. Scored the last goal of the 2021/22 season for United (6)
2. Last United manager to win a trophy with the team (4,8)
3. Top assister in the 2021/22 season (5)
5. Keeper who made his name at Burnley (3,6)
8. New Argentine left footed defender (8)
9. The mascot and a player share this name (4)
12. All time record goalscorer with 253 (6)
13. Knocked out Man United in The FA Cup in 2021/22 on penalties (13)

THE RED DEVILS

Founded: 1878
Based: Trafford, Manchester
Stadium capacity: 74,879

1
2
3
4
5
6
7
8
9
10
11
12
13
14
15
16
17

NEWCASTLE UNITED

ACROSS:

4. New signing who has represented England 8 times (4)
6. Tall striker from New Zealand (5,4)
8. Started the 2021/22 season as Newcastle manager (5,5)
11. Scored a brace in Newcastles final game of the 2021/22 season in a 2-1 win over Burnley (6)
13. English defender with a great free kick (8)
14. New left back, joined from a Premier League rival (7)

DOWN:

1. Joined from Arsenal in 2021 (7)
2. Round Newcastle were knocked out of the 2021/22 FA Cup (5)
3. Club Eddie Howe managed before joining Newcastle (11)
5. Which Arsenal player scored an own goal in Newcastle's 2-0 win against them in May 2022 (5)
7. Double-barreled French attacker who registered 5 assists in the league in 2021/22 (5,7)
9. Football pundit and Newcastle legend (4,7)
10. Brazilian who joined in January 2022 and went on to score 5 times in the league (9)
12. Won the club's player of the year in 2021/22 (9)

THE MAGPIES

Founded: 1892
Based: Newcastle upon Tyne
Stadium capacity: 52,405

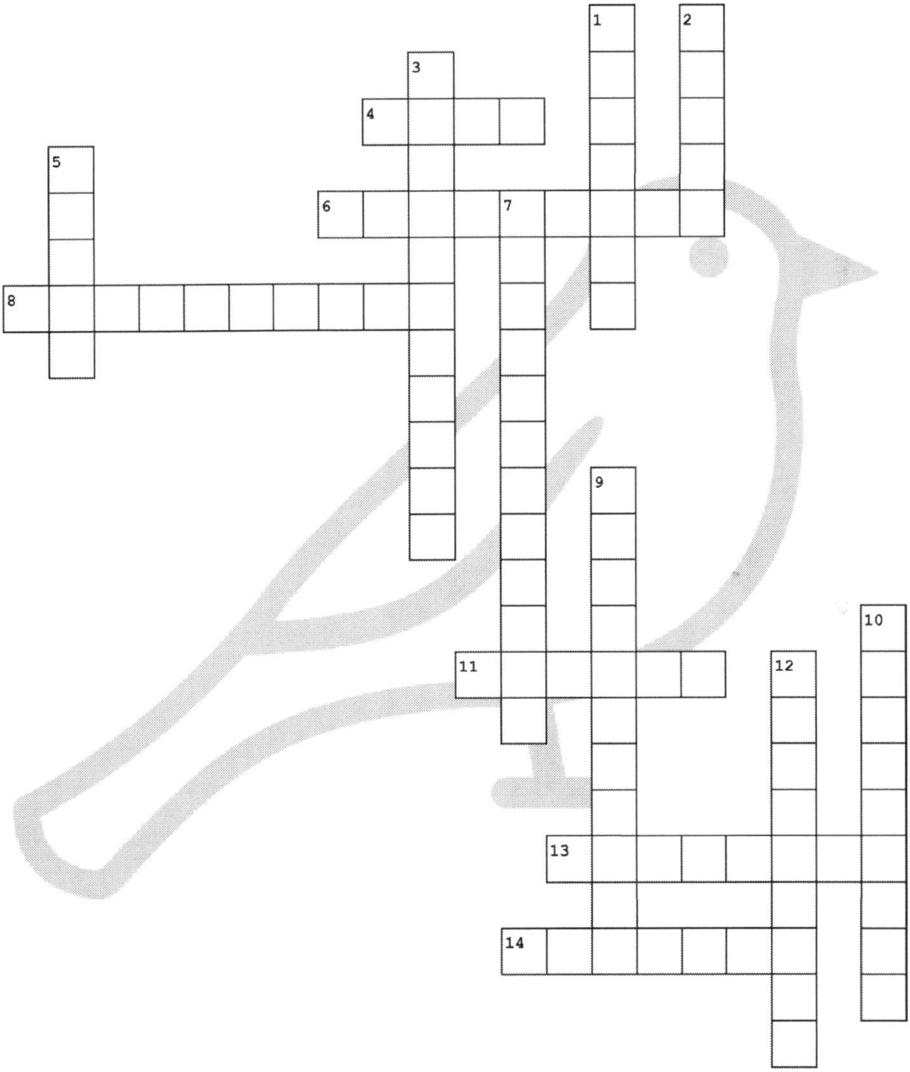
1
2
3
4
5
6
7
8
9
10
11
12
13
14

NOTTINGHAM FOREST

ACROSS:

2. Young right back signed from Liverpool (8)
4. Club that Forest beat 1-0 in the 2022 Championship playoff final (12)
10. Left back legend well remembered for missing a penalty for England in 1990 (6,6)
12. Welsh Winger and top scorer in 2021/22 (7)
13. Defender who started all but one game in the league in 2021/22 (7)
14. Defender who left for Villa in 2020/21 (4)
16. Irish midfielder who was sold in 1993 for a then record fee of £3.75 million. Now a pundit (3,5)

DOWN:

1. Scored a hat trick in 5-1 win against Swansea in 2022 (8)
3. Premier League team Forest beat 4-1 in the 2021-22 FA Cup fourth round
5. Loves to dab and has own clothing brand (7)
6. Head coach who took Forest to promotion in his first year (5,6)
7. English midfielder. Scored 8 goals in 2021/22 and featured in Championship team of the season (5)
8. Sunderland > Newcastle > Forest (4,7)
9. New forward and record signing from the Bundesliga (7)
11. Item on the clubs badge, designed originally in 1973 (4)
15. Penalty hero in the play-off semi final in 2022 (5)

FOREST

Founded: 1865
Based: West Bridgford
Stadium capacity: 30,445

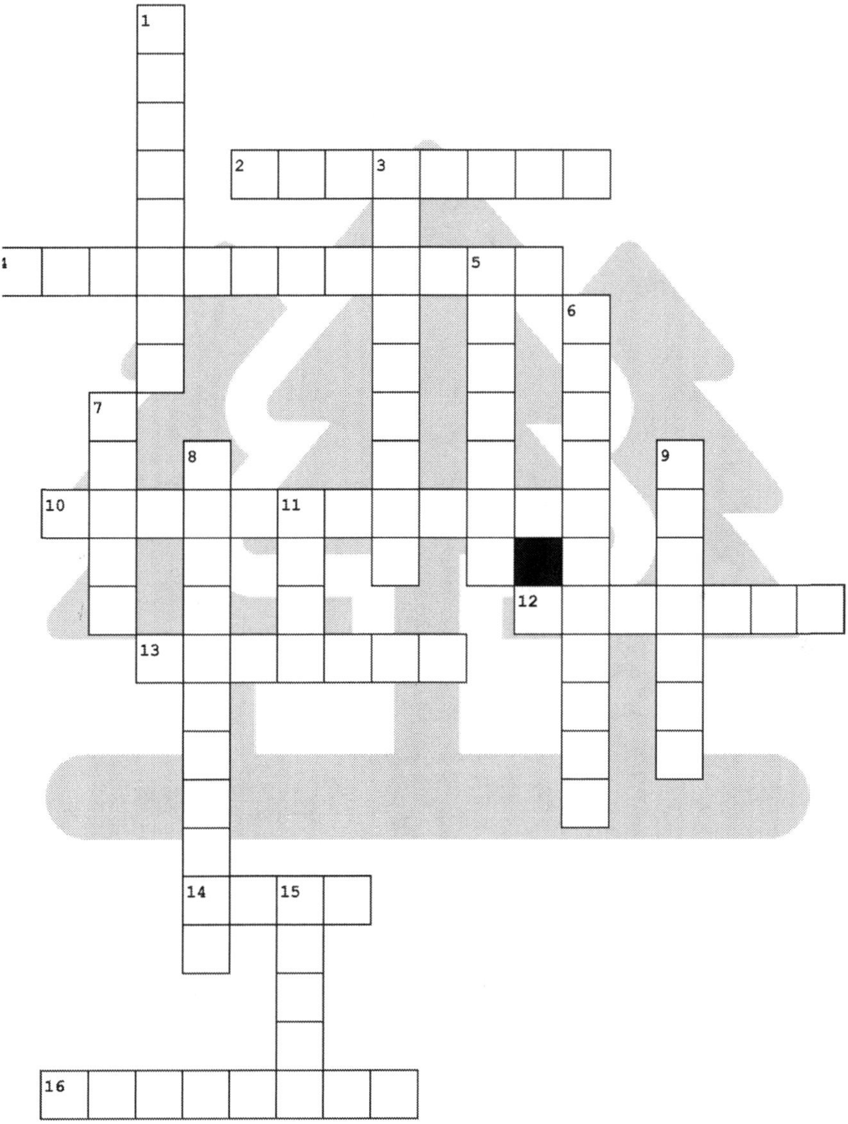
1
2
3
5
6
7
8
9
10
11
12
13
14
15
16

SOUTHAMPTON

ACROSS:

6. Saint's top scorer in 2021/22 (5,4,6)
8. Record signing for Saints in 2019. Scored 41 goals in 91 games in the league (4)
9. Exciting young fullback who joined from Chelsea (10)
12. New signing from Rangers, Joe ____ (5)
14. Scored the only goal in the win over Arsenal in April 2022 (8)

DOWN:

1. A little part-of-a-skeleton, Will ____ (9)
2. Goalkeeper who has recently joined Spurs (7)
3. Ralph Hasenhüttl took over from this manager in 2018 (6)
4. Scottish striker who joined in 2019 (5)
5. Spanish midfield enforcer (5)
7. Veteran English attacker who has four published children's books (7)
10. Saints record sale in 2017/18 (3,4)
11. Not brothers despite sharing this last name (9)
13. Birmingham > Norwich > Saints (7)

THE SAINTS

Founded: 1885
Based: Southampton
Stadium capacity: 32,384

1
2
3
4
5
6
7
8
9
10
11
12
13
14

TOTTENHAM HOTSPUR

ACROSS:

2. Left sided player that joined from Inter Milan (7)
3. Record sale back in 2013/14 at over £90million (6,4)
4. Four assists from this Irish wingback in 2021/22 (7)
6. Made an impact after signing on loan in January 2022 (10)
9. Joint golden boot winner with Mo Salah in 2021/22 with 23 goals (3)
11. Top assister for Spurs in the league in 2021/22 (5,4)
12. Central midfielder for the club and product of the Spurs youth system (5)
13. Sao Paulo > PSG > Spurs (5)
14. Ever-present in the league in 2021/22
16. New attacker, cost over £50million (11)

DOWN:

1. Knocked out Spurs in The FA Cup 5th round in 2021/22 (13)
5. Moved into their new stadium from here in 2019 (5,4,4)
7. Another nickname based on the colour of their shirts The ____ (10)
8. Type of bird on the Spurs crest (8)
10. Head coach, Conte, joined from here in 2019 (5,5)
15. English defender who moved to Portgual at 7 years old (4)

SPURS

Founded: 1882
Based: Tottenham, London
Stadium capacity: 62,850

1
2
3
4
5
6
7
8
9
10
11
12
13
14
15
16

WEST HAM

ACROSS:

2. Defender who scored the winner in a thrilling 3-2 victory against Chelsea in December 2021 (7)
4. Considered to be one of the best English midfielders (6,4)
7. Muscular Jamaican forward (7)
8. New central defender signed from Stade Rennais (6)
11. Penalty king who wade 550 appearances for West Ham before retiring in 2022 (4,5)
12. Argentinian who is nicknamed 'The Jewel' (7)
14. Knocked West Ham out of the Europa League 2021/22 semi-final (9)
15. Forever blowing ____ (7)

DOWN:

1. The first relegation of David Moyes' managerial career was with this club (10)
3. Italian magician, scored 47 goals in 118 games for West Ham in the Premier League between 1998-2003 (2,5)
5. St Etienne > Chelsea > West Ham (5)
6. Fan-favourite Ukranian attacker (10)
9. Veteran shot stopper with over 300 appearances in the Premier League (9)
10. Top scorer and creator for West Ham in 2021/22 (5)
13. Club record signing. Striker who left for Ajax in 2021 (6)

THE HAMMERS

Founded: 1895
Based: Stratford, London
Stadium capacity: 62,500

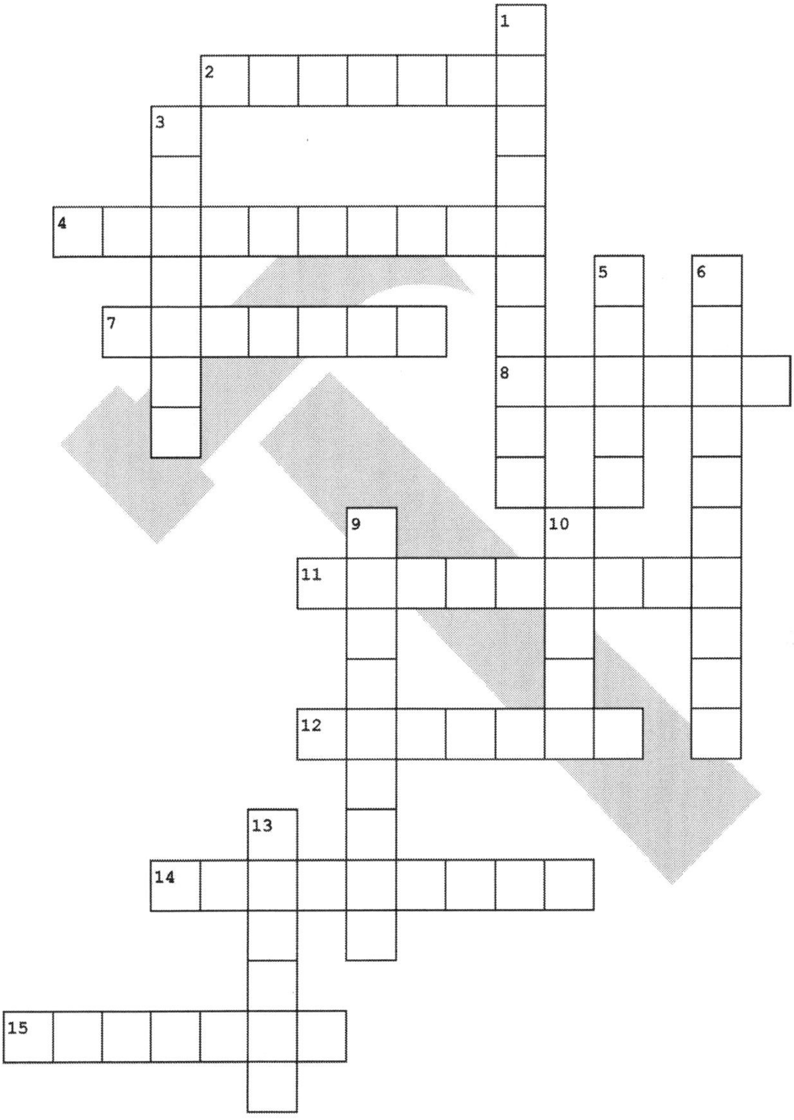
1
2
3
4
5
6
7
8
9
10
11
12
13
14
15

WOLVERHAMPTON WANDERERS

ACROSS:

2. English defender who started every Premier League game in 2021/22 (5)
5. Nickname given to Wolves from rival West Midland clubs taken from Emmerdale, The ____ (7)
6. Scored the last goal of the 2021/22 season in the 3-1 loss against Liverpool (4)
7. The first name of this towering French defender could be considered rude (5,4)
9. Wolves home stadium (8)
10. Wolves signed tenacious midfielder Ruben Neves from this club in 2017 (2,5)
12. Top scorer for Wolves in the league in 2021/22 with just 6 goals (7)
13. Number of penalties Wolves were awarded in the league in 2021/22 (3)
14. Promising youngster on loan at Anderlecht, Fabio ____ (5)

DOWN:

1. Manager, joined in June 2021 (5,4)
3. Returned to Wolves after a loan at Barcelona in the 2021/22 season (5,6)
4. Rivals. Match dubbed The Black Country Derby (4,8,6)
8. New centre back from Burnley for over £20million (7)
9. Scored in the 1-0 over Man United on 3rd January, 2022 (8)
11. Wolves have a strong relationship with this Portuguese football agent (6)

WOLVES

Founded: 1877
Based: Wolverhampton
Stadium capacity: 32,050

1
2
3
4
5
6
7
8
9
10
11
12
13
14

ANSWERS

ARSENAL

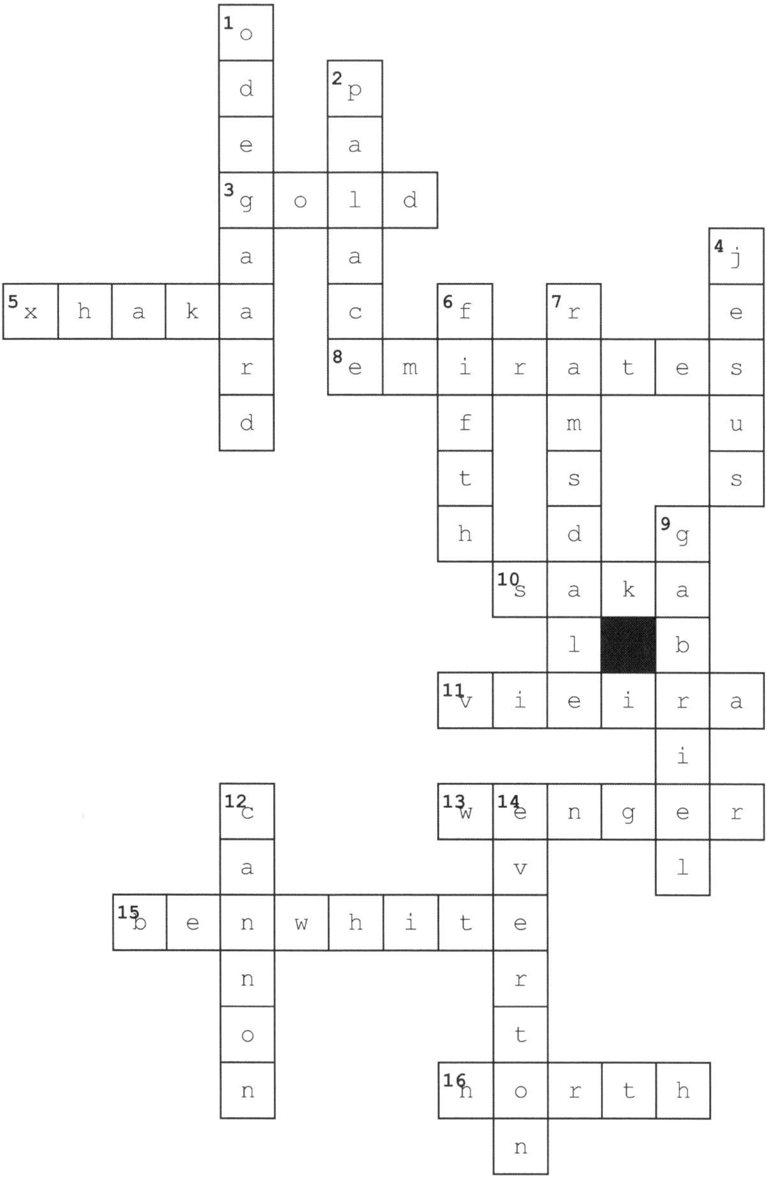

1 odegaard
2 palace
3 gold
4 jesus
5 xhaka
6 fifth
7 ramsdale
8 emirates
9 gabriel
10 saka
11 vieira
12 cannon
13 wenger
14 everton
15 benwhite
16 north

ANSWERS

ASTON VILLA

1 watkins
2 carlos
3 digne
4 mings
5 mcginn
6 coutinho
7 claret
8 birmingham
9 martinez
10 everton
11 buendía
12 hause
13 villa
14 young
15 agbonlahor
16 league

ANSWERS

BOURNEMOUTH

1 vitality
2 fredericks
3 wilson
4 travers
5 southampton
6 solanke
7 lerma
8 ake
9 parker
10 athletic
11 moore
12 dorset
13 boscombe
13 billing
14 red
15 second

ANSWERS

BRENTFORD

1 strakosha
2 griffin
3 mbeumo
4 benrahma
5 olliewatkins
6 cano
7 eight
8 frank
9 ivantoney
10 henry
11 norgaard
12 lewispotter
13 eriksen
14 janelt
jamaica

ANSWERS

BRIGHTON

1 burn
2 nint
3 crystalpalace
4 ireland
5 potter
6 genk
7 sanchez
8 five
9 welbeck
10 cook
11 caicedo
11 cucurella
12 bluewhite
13 enciso
14 amex
15 undav

ANSWERS

CHELSEA

1 masonmount
2 lukaku
3 mendy
3 mount
4 jorginho
5 gallagher
6 havertz
7 five
7 franklampard
8 reecejames
9 silva
10 kepa
11 palmeira
12 stamfordbridge
13 barkley
14 pensioners

ANSWERS

CRYSTAL PALACE

1 johnstone
2 gallagher
3 olise
4 sehurs
5 wilfriedzaha
6 patrickvieira
7 benteke
8 edouard
9 white
10 tyrick
11 mcarthur
12 doucoure
13 guehi
14 five
15 zaha

ANSWERS

EVERTON

1 lukaku
2 lampard
3 duncanferguson
4 tarkowski
5 gordon
5 goodison
6 vandebeek
7 richarlison
8 merseyside
9 dog
10 sigurdsson
11 rafabenitez
12 keane
13 sunderland

ANSWERS

FULHAM

1 palhinha
2 cairney
3 newcastle
4 seri
5 andreaspereira
6 ffc
7 aleksandar
8 marcosilva
9 saha
10 ream
11 mitrovic
12 wilson
13 scottparker
14 seven

ANSWERS

LEEDS UNITED

1 arsenal
2 manchestercity
3 raphina
4 home
5 danieljames
6 bielsa
7 aaronson
8 one
9 meslier
10 harrison
11 ayling
12 ellandroad
13 jamesmilner
14 marsch

ANSWERS

LEICESTER

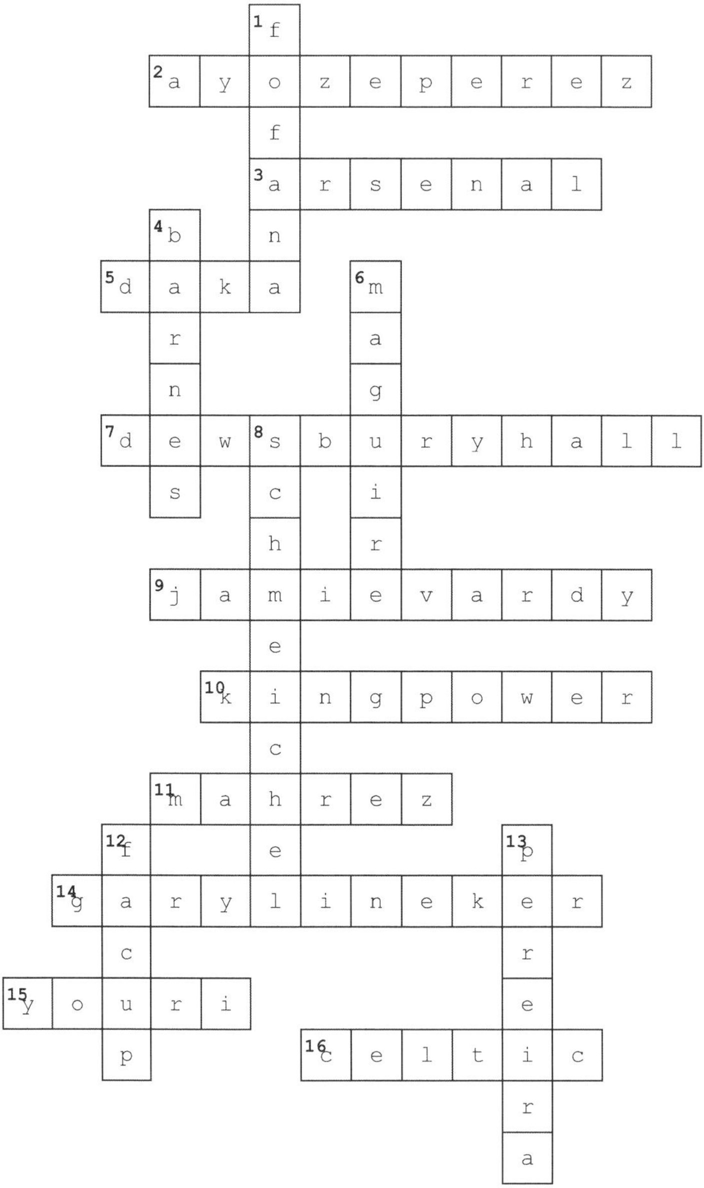
1 fofana
2 ayozeperez
3 arsenal
4 barnes
5 daka
6 maguire
7 dewsburyhall
8 schmeichel
9 jamievardy
10 kingpower
11 mahrez
12 facup
13 pereira
14 garylineker
15 youri
16 celtic

ANSWERS

LIVERPOOL

1 man
2 carvalho
3 darwinnunez
4 kelleher
5 luisdiaz
6 virgilvandijk
7 bayernmunich
8 coutinho
9 tsimikas
10 fabinho
11 jamesmilner
12 ianrush
13 alexanderarnold
14 junior
15 brendanrodgers
16 chelsea
17 mosalah

ANSWERS

MANCHESTER CITY

1 jackgrealish
2 foden
3 bluemoon
4 markhughes
5 gabrieljesus
6 steve
7 etihad
8 erlinghaaland
9 debruyne
10 aguero
11 fou
12 sterling
13 gundogan
14 phillips
15 bayernmunich
16 cancelo

ANSWERS

MANCHESTER UNITED

1 varane
2 josemourinho
3 pogba
4 ronaldo
5 tomheaton
6 degea
7 beckham
8 martínez
9 fred
10 christianeriksen
11 theatreofdreams
12 rooney
13 middlesbrough
14 mcfred
15 glazers
16 utrecht
17 garnacho

ANSWERS

NEWCASTLE UNITED

1 willock
2 third
3 bournemouth
4 pope
5 white
6 chriswood
7 saintmaximin
8 stevebruce
9 alanshearer
10 guimaraes
11 wilson
12 joelinton
13 trippier
14 target

ANSWERS

NOTTINGHAM FOREST

1 surridge
2 williams
3 leicester
4 huddersfield
5 lingard
6 stevecooper
7 yates
8 jackcolback
9 awoniyi
10 stuartpearce
11 tree
12 johnson
13 mckenna
14 cash
15 samba
16 roykeane

ANSWERS

SOUTHAMPTON

1 smallbone
2 forster
3 hughes
4 adams
5 romeu
6 jameswardprowse
7 walcott
8 ings
9 livramento
10 vandijk
11 armstrong
12 aribo
13 redmond
14 bednarek

ANSWERS

TOTTENHAM HOTSPUR

1 middlesbrough
2 perisic
3 garethbale
4 doherty
5 whitehartlane
6 kulusevski
7 lilywhites
8 cockerel
9 son
10 intermilan
11 harrykane
12 winks
13 moura
14 lloris
15 dier
16 richarlison

ANSWERS

WEST HAM

1 sunderland
2 masuaku
3 dicanio
4 declanrice
5 zouma
6 yarmolenko
7 antonio
8 aguerd
9 fabianski
10 bowen
11 marknoble
12 lanzini
13 haller
14 frankfurt
15 bubbles

ANSWERS

WOLVERHAMPTON WANDERERS

1 brunolage
2 coady
3 adamatraore
4 westbromwichalbion
5 dingles
6 neto
7 willyboly
8 collins
9 molineux
9 moutinho
10 fcporto
11 mendes
12 jimenez
13 one
14 silva

THANK YOU

If you enjoyed this crossword puzzle book, please recommend it to your friends and family to help support the football-mad fans who made it.

You can find our other books by searching for Creative Contributors on Amazon.

Or if you're a fantasy football fan, check out our FPL Journal!

FANTASY PREMIER LEAGUE JOURNAL

The ultimate Fantasy Premier League Journal for the season.

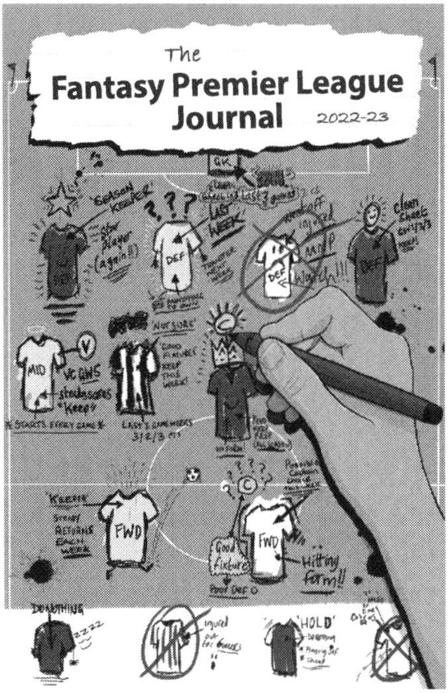
The
Fantasy Premier League
Journal
2022-23

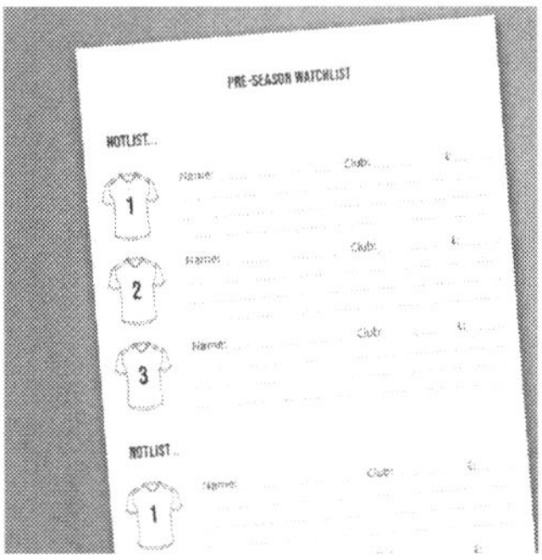
PRE-SEASON WATCHLIST
HOTLIST...
NOTLIST...

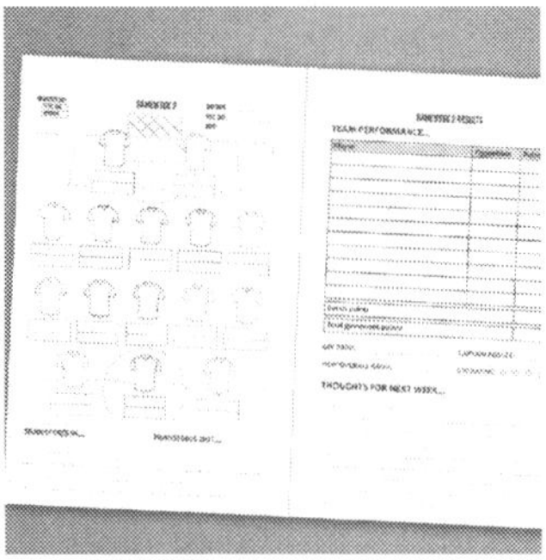

AVAILABLE ON AMAZON

Manufactured by Amazon.ca
Bolton, ON

36522309R00037